Panning for GOLD

Paul Mason

www.raintreepublishers.co.uk
Visit our website to find out more information about **Raintree** books.

To order:
- ☎ Phone 44 (0) 1865 888112
- 🖹 Send a fax to 44 (0) 1865 314091
- 🖥 Visit the Raintree Bookshop at **www.raintreepublishers.co.uk** to browse our catalogue and order online.

First published in Great Britain by Raintree,
Halley Court, Jordan Hill, Oxford OX2 8EJ,
part of Harcourt Education.
Raintree is a registered trademark of Harcourt
Education Ltd.

Editorial: Nancy Dickmann and Catherine Veitch
Design: Philippa Jenkins and Q2A Creative
Illustrations: Mark Preston pp.10, 26, 27. Jeff Edwards
pp.4, 5, 8.
Picture Research: Ruth Blair
Production: Sevy Ribierre

Originated by Modern Age
Printed and bound in China by Leo Paper Group

ISBN 978 1 4062 0738 5 (hardback)
12 11 10 09 08
10 9 8 7 6 5 4 3 2 1

ISBN 978 1 4062 0752 1 (paperback)
12 11 10 09 08
10 9 8 7 6 5 4 3 2 1

**British Library Cataloguing in Publication
Data**
Mason, Paul, 1967-
Panning for gold. - (Fusion)
1. Mixtures - Juvenile literature
2. Solution (Chemistry) Juvenile literature
I. Title   541.3'4
A full catalogue record for this book is available from
the British Library.

Acknowledgements
The publishers would like to thank the following for
permission to reproduce photographs: Alamy pp.**10**
(plainpicture GmbH & Co. KG), **16** (INTERFOTO
Pressebildagentur), **23** (AA World Travel Library);
Corbis pp.**12-13**, **15** (Guy Motil), **14-15** (Museum
of History and Industry), **21**, **29** (Dave G. Houser);
Corbis (Bettmann) pp.**5**, **7**, **9**, **19**, **22-23**, **24**;
Science Photo Library pp.**4-5** (Dr. Morley Read), **17**
(Photography collection, Mirian and Ira D. Wallach
Divison Of Art, Prints and Photographs/Humanities
and Social Sciences Library/New York Public Library).

Cover photograph of a man holding a pan containing
nuggets of gold reproduced with permission of Getty
Images/Stone.

Every effort has been made to contact copyright
holders of any material reproduced in this book. Any
omissions will be rectified in subsequent printings if
notice is given to the publishers.

The publishers would like to thank Nancy Harris and
Harold Pratt for their assistance with the preparation
of this book.

Contents

Some words are printed in bold, **like this**. You can find out what they mean on page 30. You can also look in the box at the bottom of the page where they first appear.

"Gold from the American River!"

One day, something exciting happened on the streets of San Francisco. San Francisco is a city in California in the United States of America. A local man named Samuel Brannan was shouting. The year was 1848.

Brannan was holding a small glass bottle in the air. It was filled with gold! "Gold!" he shouted, "Gold from the American River!" People quickly crowded around Brannan.

There had already been talk of gold being discovered nearby. Now people knew it was true!

People rushed to California from all over the world. They hoped to get rich by looking for gold. This was called **prospecting**.

Imagine what it must have been like to set off for California. People had to leave their family and friends.

Gold! In 1849, just one nugget could make a man rich. A nugget is a piece of gold.

gold nugget

4

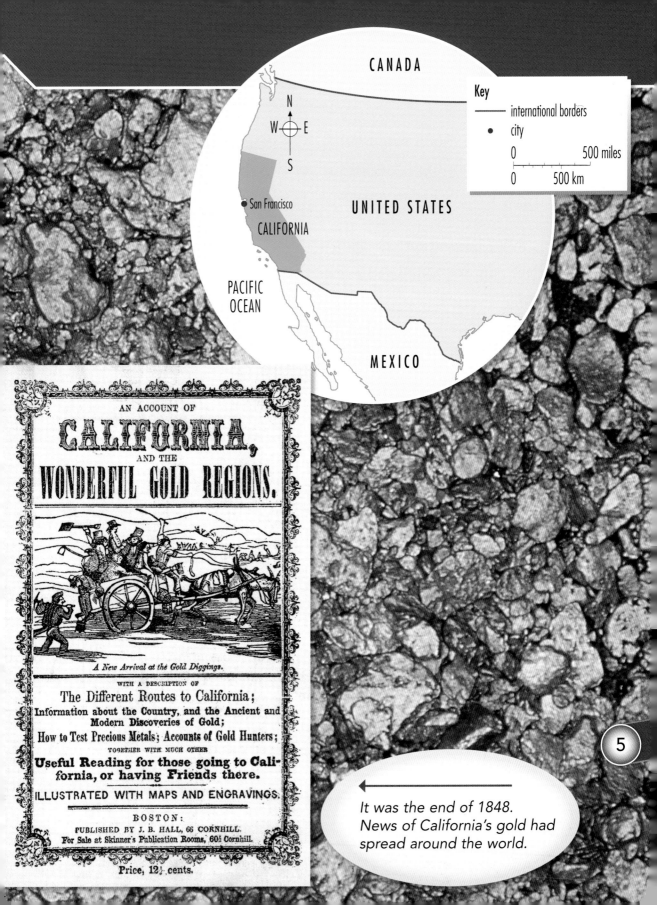

CANADA

N
W · E
S

Key
——— international borders
• city

0 _____ 500 miles
0 ___ 500 km

UNITED STATES

San Francisco

CALIFORNIA

PACIFIC
OCEAN

MEXICO

AN ACCOUNT OF
CALIFORNIA,
AND THE
WONDERFUL GOLD REGIONS.

A New Arrival at the Gold Diggings.

WITH A DESCRIPTION OF

The Different Routes to California;

Information about the Country, and the Ancient and
Modern Discoveries of Gold;

How to Test Precious Metals; Accounts of Gold Hunters;

TOGETHER WITH MUCH OTHER

**Useful Reading for those going to Cali-
fornia, or having Friends there.**

ILLUSTRATED WITH MAPS AND ENGRAVINGS.

BOSTON:
PUBLISHED BY J. B. HALL, 66 CORNHILL.
For Sale at Skinner's Publication Rooms, 60½ Cornhill.

Price, 12½ cents.

5

*It was the end of 1848.
News of California's gold had
spread around the world.*

Gold from water

What did Brannan mean when he shouted, "Gold from the American River"? How can you get gold from a river?

Gold was first found at a place called Sutter's Mill. Sutter's Mill was next to the American River.

One day, a mill worker was looking at the river water. He spotted a speck of shiny metal. The metal turned out to be gold!

The water of the American River was a **mixture**. A mixture is made of two or more things mixed together. The river water had little flecks of gold mixed in. There was also lots of mud, sand, and gravel in the mixture.

Gold fact!

Most gold-hunters began arriving in California in 1849. They are known as "49ers". They were also known as **prospectors**.

mixture combination of two or more things
prospector person who looks for valuable things in the ground
separate take out, or split into different parts

This 49er hoped to **separate** gold from the river water and mud.

7

The rush to California

People rushed to California from far-away places. Many people travelled across North America. They travelled from the East Coast to the West Coast.

At first the journey from the East Coast went well. The 49ers looked forward to reaching California. They looked forward to making their fortunes. Soon things began to go wrong.

Some 49ers did not bring enough clean water. They were forced to drink dirty water from streams and ponds. The water had **germs** that caused disease.

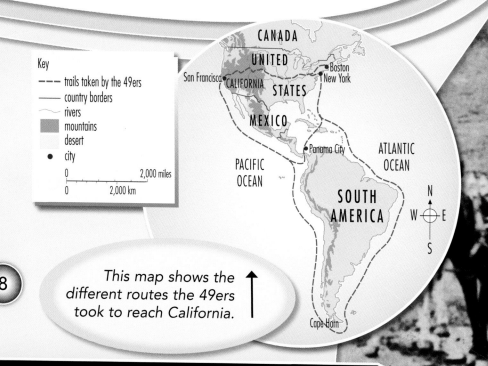

Key
- - - - trails taken by the 49ers
───── country borders
∼∼∼ rivers
▨ mountains
☐ desert
• city

0   2,000 miles
0   2,000 km

CANADA
UNITED
STATES
San Francisco • CALIFORNIA
• Boston
• New York
MEXICO
• Panama City
PACIFIC
OCEAN
ATLANTIC
OCEAN
SOUTH
AMERICA
Cape Horn

N
W ⊕ E
S

This map shows the different routes the 49ers took to reach California.

8

germ tiny creature that causes illness

A group of 49ers on their long journey to the goldfields.

Gold fact!

It was almost 4,828 kilometres (3,000 miles) from the East Coast to California. Many 49ers walked most of the way!

The pond water was a **mixture**. This mixture did not contain gold! It was a mixture of clean water and unhealthy germs. Many travellers became ill. Some even died.

Separating mixtures

Mixtures were an important part of life as a 49er. Mixtures of water and gold made him rich. But mixtures of water and **germs** made him sick.

Remember the gold that was taken out of the American River water? This gold had been **separated** out of the river-water mixture. The things that make up a mixture can always be separated out again.

It was very hot. The 49ers would have needed to drink plenty of water.

Some travellers tried to separate out the germs from their water. They stretched a cloth over a bucket. Next they poured the water through the cloth. The cloth acted as a **filter**. A filter is a barrier. It lets some things through but not others. Filtering is one way of separating out parts of a mixture.

Here, a cloth filter separates dirt from water.

jug

dirty water

dirt trapped by filter

cloth

bucket

cleaner water pours into bucket

Water problems

Filtering the water did not work. The cloth trapped the large parts of the **mixture**. It let the smaller ones through. The tiny **germs** were too small to be trapped by the cloth.

Some other substances also got through the cloth filter. They were a type of mixture called a **solution**. A solution is made of things that have mixed together very well. You cannot see the separate parts of a solution.

Think of sugar mixed into a hot drink. Once you have stirred it in, the sugar disappears from sight. You know it is there because you can taste it. But you cannot see the sugar. The drink is a solution.

Gold fact!

As they travelled to California the 49ers needed water. They were so thirsty they paid around £50 per glass!

solution type of mixture where the different parts

Using a cloth as a filter does not work on the tiny germs. It will not work on a solution either. Luckily for the miners, there are other ways to **separate** solutions.

These 49ers used oxen to carry goods to the goldfields. **Prospectors** came from all round the world.

Sailing the salty sea

Some people travelled to California by sea. Seawater is a **mixture**. It is a mixture of salt and water. The mixture is called a **solution**. You cannot see the salt in the water.

When a liquid warms up, it starts to turn into a gas. A gas has no fixed shape. Air is a gas. **Evaporation** is when a liquid turns to gas. Evaporation is one way to **separate** out parts of a solution.

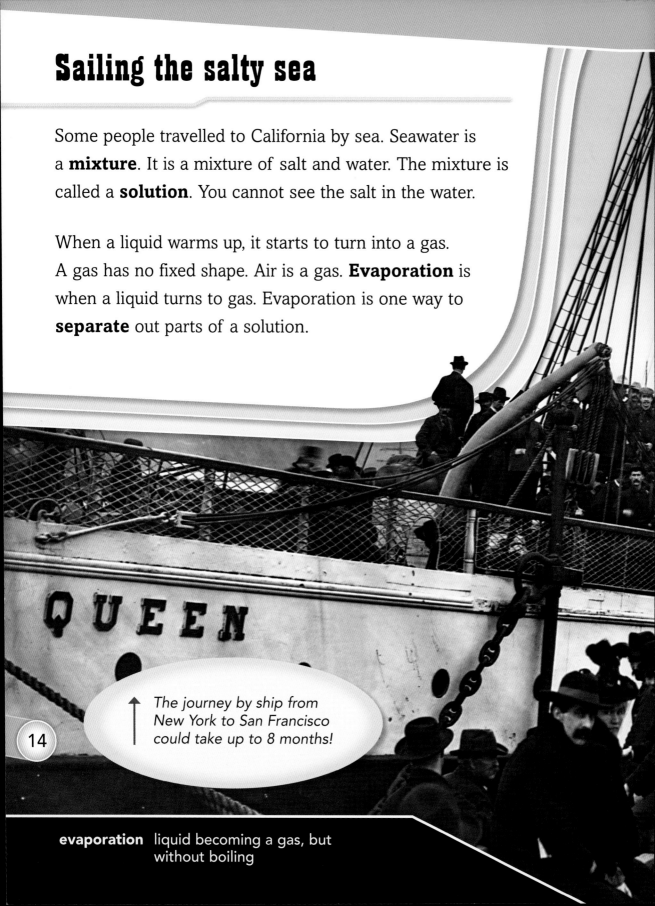

↑ *The journey by ship from New York to San Francisco could take up to 8 months!*

evaporation liquid becoming a gas, but without boiling

This is a picture of the stormy seas near Cape Horn. Some people sailed through them to get to San Francisco (see page 8).

When the Sun heats the water in the sea, the water begins to evaporate. It becomes a gas in the air. But the salt does not evaporate. It is left behind. This is what causes the sea to be salty.

Evaporation is one way that the parts of a solution can be separated out. The water separates from the salt.

15

San Francisco

The 49ers finally reached California. They bought pans and **sieves**. These were for sorting gold from the rocks and mud of the river.

The 49ers also needed a tent and bedroll for sleeping. Finally, they bought cooking gear and supplies.

Gold fact!

A very large piece of gold was found during the Gold Rush. It weighed 88 kilograms (195 pounds). That's more than a grown man!

Many of the stores along this street sold equipment to **prospectors**. Selling equipment was big business. It made some people millionaires.

A 49er has his gold weighed in town. He would then agree a price for selling it.

Selling supplies to miners was big business.

Here are some of the prices from the goldfields:

- bag of sugar: about £1.05
- bag of coffee: about £2.11
- cooked meal: about £13.18

These prices were very high. In other places a bag of sugar would have cost a few pence. A meal would have cost about 13 pence.

To the goldfields!

The trail was hard on the 49ers. Most of them wore the same dirty clothes for the whole journey. They sweated in the hot weather. Their clothes dried out at night. White rings were left behind. The rings showed the edge of where their clothes had got wet.

These white marks were from the 49ers' sweat. Their sweat was a **mixture** of salt and **minerals**. Salt and minerals come from the body. Sweat is the type of mixture known as a **solution**. The salt and minerals cannot be seen in the water.

The sweat was dried out by the 49ers' body heat. The water from the sweat **evaporated** into the air. The water turned into gas. The salty marks were left behind on the cloth. Evaporation **separated** out parts of the solution.

By the time the 49ers reached the goldfields, they were quite smelly.

Searching for gold was hot, dirty work.

The mining camp

Some miners' camps had very worrying names. They included "Gouge Eye" and "Hell's Delight"! But there were places with better names. One was called "Angels' Camp".

When they arrived, the 49ers put up their tents. Then the bedroll and the rest of their equipment went in. After setting up camp, they were ready for some coffee. This involved more **mixtures** (two or more things mixed together).

See if you can count how many mixtures were in a 49er's coffee:

1) First, he added coffee **grounds** to water.

2) Then he boiled the water.

3) The hot coffee was poured into a mug. The 49er was careful not to pour in any of the grounds. They tasted horrible!

4) He added sugar to the hot coffee and stirred it in.

The answers are on page 28.

A miners' camp at Deadwood, South Dakota, U.S.A..

Gold fact!

Some 49ers did not bring equipment. They ended up paying a high price for equipment. At the camps, **prospecting** gear could cost more than £100!

Life as a 49er

A 49er's first day at the goldfields must have been very exciting. At last, there was a chance to head for the river. They could find some gold!

The 49ers used their **sieves** to find gold. They scooped up water, mud, dirt, and rocks from the river.

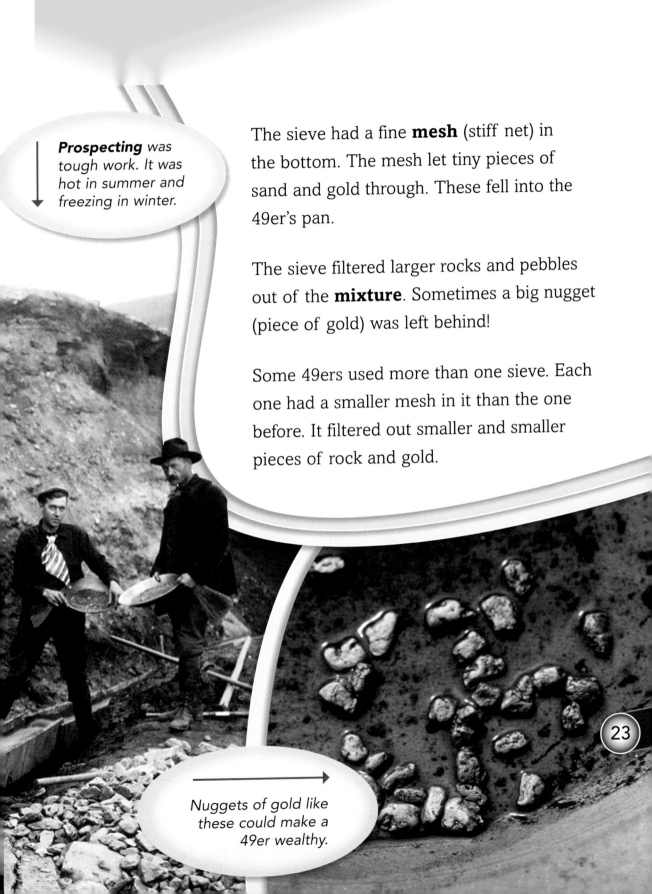

Prospecting was tough work. It was hot in summer and freezing in winter.

The sieve had a fine **mesh** (stiff net) in the bottom. The mesh let tiny pieces of sand and gold through. These fell into the 49er's pan.

The sieve filtered larger rocks and pebbles out of the **mixture**. Sometimes a big nugget (piece of gold) was left behind!

Some 49ers used more than one sieve. Each one had a smaller mesh in it than the one before. It filtered out smaller and smaller pieces of rock and gold.

23

Nuggets of gold like these could make a 49er wealthy.

Many people crossed the Pacific Ocean during the California Gold Rush. They came from China.

panning swirling a mixture in water, in a shallow pan, to separate pieces

Panning for gold

After filtering there could be small pieces of gold left in the pan. It was time to start **panning**!

1) In the bottom of the pan were tiny pieces of gold, rock, and mud. These had passed through the filter.

2) The 49ers added water to this **mixture**. They swirled it around. They made sure the water swished over the edge of the pan. The lightest bits of rock and mud swished out with the water.

3) When all the water was gone, the 49ers added more water. Then the swishing started again.

4) In the end, all the mud and tiny bits of rock had gone. Only gold was left in the pan.

How did this work? Turn the page to find out!

Gold — heavy metal!

Panning separates gold from other things in the 49er's pan. Panning works because gold is heavier than other things in the **mixture**. These diagrams explain what happens when you pan for gold.

At the end of their first day, most 49ers had a few specks of gold. They were usually tiny specks. The 49ers probably didn't mind. Tomorrow, they might find the largest nugget (piece of gold) yet seen!

The **prospector** swirls water around his pan. He tips it slightly. Each swirl spills a small amount of water.

1. When you first add water, the gold is mixed in with everything else.

2. The water swirls around. A mixture of water and dirt spills out. The heavier rocks and gold are left behind.

3. Now the dirt has gone. You swirl a tiny bit harder. The smaller bits of rock swish out of the side of your pan.

4. The bits of gold are heavier than everything else. They have slowly sunk to the bottom of the pan. Everything else has been swished out. All that is left is the gold!

Prospector's diary

Imagine another gold rush happened tomorrow. Would you be ready to head off in the hope of striking it rich?

You would have many adventures on your trip. Write a diary about these adventures.

Here are some things to think about when planning your journey:

1) Gold rushes often happen along mountain rivers. Which mountains might your gold rush happen in?

2) Use an atlas to plan your route. What kind of ground will you have to cross to get to the goldfields? Will it be hot, cold, wet, or dry?

3) Do you need to take camping gear with you? Where will you live when you get to the goldfield?

4) What equipment will you need? Will you take a **sieve** or a pan?

Quiz answers

These are the different **mixtures** involved in making coffee on page 20:

1) Adding coffee **grounds** to water makes the first mixture.

2) When the mixture is boiled, a small amount of coffee **dissolves** in the water. You can no longer see the coffee grounds. This must be a **solution**.

3) Pouring the coffee out and leaving the grounds behind **separated** out the grounds.

4) Adding sugar made the third mixture. You cannot see the sugar once it has dissolved. It is another solution.

Even today, people are
still **panning** for gold. ↑

Glossary

dissolve make into part of a liquid solution. The sugar you stir into a hot drink dissolves and becomes part of a solution.

evaporation liquid becoming a gas, but without boiling. If you put a plate of water outside on a hot, sunny day, it will disappear by evening. The water has evaporated.

filter barrier that only small things can pass through. A fishing net is a kind of filter – small fish can get through it, but bigger fish are caught.

germ tiny creature that causes illness. Germs are so small that they cannot be seen except with a microscope.

grounds small pieces of chopped-up coffee

mesh criss-cross pattern with holes in it, like a net

mineral natural material found in the ground. For example, coal, salt, or gold!

mixture combination of two or more things. For example, when you stir oats into milk and heat it up, you make a mixture called porridge.

panning swirling a mixture in water, in a shallow pan, to separate pieces

prospecting looking for valuable things in the ground. The 49ers were prospecting for gold, but prospectors could also look for silver or diamonds.

prospector person who looks for valuable things in the ground

separate take out, or split into different parts. Panning for gold separates the gold from whatever it is mixed with.

sieve short, wide wooden tube, with a criss-cross mesh in the bottom. Sieves are used to separate small objects from larger ones.

solution type of mixture where the different parts cannot be seen. Stirring sugar into a hot drink makes a solution. The sugar "disappears", even though you can tell it is there through taste.

Want to know more?

Books to read

- *California Gold Rush*, Peter Roop (Scholastic Paperbacks, 2002)

- *Children of the Gold Rush*, Claire Rudolf Murphy and Jane G. Haigh (Alaska Northwest Books, 2001)

- *The Forty-Niners: The Story of the California Gold Rush*, Cynthia Mercati (Perfection Learning, 2002)

Websites

- www.malakoff.com/goldcountry/campmap.htm
  Click on the names of old Californian mining camps that are now towns.
  Find out their history.

- www.isu.edu/~trinmich/funfacts.html
  Fun information about the Gold Rush, including the "wind wagon" – a
  kite-powered wagon for getting to California as fast as possible (it didn't work)!

- www.museumca.org/goldrush/fever01.html
  Information on all aspects of the California Gold Rush.

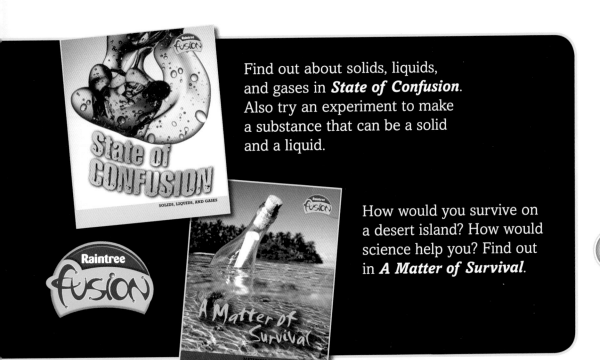

Find out about solids, liquids, and gases in **State of Confusion**. Also try an experiment to make a substance that can be a solid and a liquid.

How would you survive on a desert island? How would science help you? Find out in **A Matter of Survival**.

Index